The Let's Talk Library™

Let's Talk About
Moving to a New Place

Diana Star Helmer

The Rosen Publishing Group's
PowerKids Press™
New York

Published in 1999 by The Rosen Publishing Group, Inc.
29 East 21st Street, New York, NY 10010

First Edition

Book Design: Erin Mckenna

Photo Illustrations: Cover and all photo illustrations by Seth Dinnerman.

Helmer, Diana Star, 1962–.
    Let's talk about moving to a new place / by Diana Star Helmer.
        p. cm. — (The let's talk library)
    Includes index.
    Summary: Discusses some of the feelings that moving from one place
    to another may cause and how to adjust.
    ISBN 0-8239-5194-4
    1. Moving, Household—Juvenile literature. I. Title. II. Series.
TX307.H458 1998
648'.9—dc21   97–46975
                                                              CIP
                                                              AC

Manufactured in the United States of America

Table of Contents

Something Old, Something New

Tom was in bed with his favorite blanket and bear, but he couldn't sleep. His new house smelled funny. Tom was used to the smells in his old house. Tom didn't recognize the shadows in his new room. He also didn't recognize the sounds in his new house.

"Dad," Tom said as his father passed his room. "Everything is different here!"

"Things will feel strange for a while," Dad said. "But we will all get used to our new home."

5

◀ Getting used to a new home may take some time.

Change Isn't So Strange

Families move for different reasons. Maybe houses become too small as children grow up. New jobs or schools might be far away, and families have to move closer. Or maybe families change and part of a family moves away. Moving always means change. But you already know about change. You go to a friend's house to play, or you start a new class at school. And you see different people at each place.

Moving and change can be scary. But you and your family can help each other through it. ▶

Knowing Your Feelings

Moving can mix up the things in your house and your room. Moving can mix up your feelings too. Part of you may feel sad about leaving the places and people you know. But part of you might be excited thinking about new friends and new things to do. Once you get used to those feelings, they won't be so new anymore. Part of being **comfortable** (KUMF-ter-bul) in your new home is knowing your new feelings.

◀ Helping out with your own things during the move can also help you to figure out your feelings.

A Place You Know

You can start learning about your new home even before you move. Ask your family about what your new home will be like. Ask your teacher or neighbor if she knows someone who lives near your new home. Ask your mom or dad to help you look on the **Internet** (IN-ter-net) for facts about your new town. You can ask your librarian to help you. The more you know about your new place, the sooner it will feel like home.

Using a map, you can show your old friends ▶
where your new home is going to be.

Packed and Organized

Organizing (OR-guh-ny-zing) your things will also make your move easier. When things are in order they are easier to find. Ask your parents to help pack the boxes with your clothes and toys. Put labels on your boxes. Make a list of what's in each box. But most important, keep something special with you during the move. When Tom moved to his new home, his favorite bear sat on his lap as his family drove to the new house. And even before the boxes were unpacked, the bear made Tom's new room feel more like home.

◄ Keeping track of your stuff will make it easier for you to unpack and get settled in your new home.

13

Good-bye Isn't Forever

Leaving your favorite room and friends may be hard. But moving into a new room and making new friends is exciting.

You might think you are leaving your friends behind. But your friends are part of you. You have played together and had fun together, and you can still be friends. You can write letters or talk to them on the phone. You can even plan special visits to see your old friends.

Remember: It may be a while before you see your old friends again. But they're still your friends, no matter what. ▶

Showing Feelings

Moving will mean changes for everyone in your family. You might wonder about making new friends, or if the new schoolwork will be hard, or if your new teacher will be nice. Grown-ups worry about new friends and new jobs too. And everyone has to say good-bye. Many of these changes can be sad. You might show that you're sad by being mad. You might cry. Feeling this way is okay. Giving yourself some time to get used to the changes and your feelings will help as you move.

◀ Talking about your feelings with someone you trust can make moving easier.

17

Making Friends

For some people, it's easy to make friends. Other people may feel shy about meeting new people. You might be worried that your new classmates won't like you. It might feel strange at first to be away from your old friends. But give it some time. Join in a game on the playground or share your dessert with someone in your class. Before you know it, you'll have some fun, new friends.

It is actually easier than you think to ▶ talk to new people. Just be yourself.

Different But the Same

You probably feel very comfortable in your old home. You know where everything is and things feel **familiar** (fuh-MIL-yer). At first, you may not feel as comfortable in your new home. But remember, the most important things in your home stay the same. The clothes you wear, the special things you have, and most important the people who love you are there, just like always.

◄ Even though things might look and feel different in your new home, it's still your home and your family.

You Are Home

When you move, there is always something you can't take with you. Maybe it's the room that you slept in or a tree in your old backyard. But those special things will always be in your **memory** (MEM-or-ee). Your memories make you a special person. Nobody else has your memories. You can **cherish** (CHAYR-ish) your memories by drawing pictures or writing stories about places and times that you care about. That way, you can love your old home and your new home at the same time.

22

Glossary

cherish (CHAYR-ish) To care deeply about something.

comfortable (KUMF-ter-bul) Feeling no pain.

familiar (fuh-MIL-yer) Well-known to you.

Internet (IN-ter-net) Facts and information gathered from all over the world that can be found on a computer with a modem.

memory (MEM-or-ee) The part of your mind that remembers things.

organizing (OR-guh-ny-zing) Putting things in order.

Index